P
Y
R
A
M
I
D

Authors
Literary Agent
Publishers
Publicist
Marketer

TABLE OF CONTENTS

Author

Before Submitting:
- Become part of a critique group.
- Get feedback on your work.
- Agents do not want to be your first read.
- Get your book to be as perfect as possible before submitting it.
- Set realistic goals for your book.
- Separate your dreams from your goals.

The Manuscript:
- Proof read your work, and proof read your query letters.
- Don't submit a working version of your novel. You must have a finished book.
- Don't send chapters with a synopsis, or ideas. FINISH YOUR BOOK!
- Format correctly. A correct format consists of double spaced pages; 12 point font; normal margins; and page numbers.

The Query Letter:
- Keep your query letter to one page only, it should consist of at least 3 paragraphs. The first paragraph should explain why you are choosing this agent. The second paragraph should be a summary of your project, and the third paragraph should be your credentials. Your project summary is a teaser, it does not have to tell everything that happens in the book.
- Present yourself in the query letter professionally. The agent wants to make sure that you will not embarrass them or hurt their reputation. Keep in mind you are being interviewed by the agent, just as if you were sitting in front of him or her.
- Personalize your query. The agent wants to know why you have picked them Mention your research, or that you met them at a conference, etc.
- Get to the point, be upbeat and interesting, be positive, professional, and concise.
- Give a sense of where your book fits into the market.

AUTHOR

Submissions:

- Always present your work professionally!
- Always, always, always read the submission guidelines of the agency. Be sure you have read them carefully! Follow the guidelines.

When You Get a Bite:

- Get excited!   Be Professional!
- Re-familiarize yourself with that agent's agency and list. You may have submitted to multiple people and forgotten what they have done.
- Prepare questions. Some questions that will show you've done your homework will include: What is your working style? Do you prefer to communicate via email or telephone? What is your transparency with submissions to editors? How often should I expect to hear from you? Etc.
- Enjoy the journey!

DOs	DON'Ts
• Do research on prospective agents and make informed decisions.	• Don't mass e-mail agents one general "Dear Agent" query.
• Do follow submission guidelines to a T, as best you can.	• Don't send "goodies" or "research material" to prospective agents.
• Do personalize your queries.	

Literary Agent

Literary Agent – is someone who represents writers and their written works to publishers, theatrical producers and film producers and assists in the sale and deal negotiation of the same. Many well-know, powerful, and lucrative publishing houses (such as the big six) are generally less open than smaller publishers to non-agent submissions.

A client typically establishes relationships with an agent through querying. A query is an unsolicited proposal for representation, either for a finished work or unfinished work.

Advantages
- Connecting authors with publishers
- Contract negotiation
- Ensuring payment of royalties
- Acting as a mediator if there are problems between the author and the publisher

A literary agent is a person who totally represents the author in everything they do. Once the author has written a book they need someone to find the right publisher for them, in order to exploit the rights derived from the copyright of the work. The book suddenly becomes another kind of thing which the author is responsible for, but essentially the book has its own life so a literary agent comes along and says, "I think we can sell this in film, or in France, Germany, America and Italy" and exploits the rights in that. Also, a literary agent is there to help an author with their career, to talk about their choices they make about the next novel, about where they're going in novels or non-fiction. There are two jobs a literary agent has. One is more social, which is understanding what is going on in the author's life, working out their career management, and the other is the work, how best to get this work out to the most amount of people in the best possible way.

What are the advantages of having an agent?

There are lots of advantages of having a literary agent. The publishing relationship with an author can be about the book, and not necessarily about the person. If you deliver a great book to a publisher, they'll love the book, but if you deliver a not so great book, they might then move on. You need somebody who's going to be on your side, who's a partner in your business. There's also the fact that, even if you were very savvy, you knew exactly who you wanted to publish your book, and, for some

LITERARY AGENT

unknown reason, you knew the market rate of your novel, which does take years to understand, do you want to be spending a lot of your time on emails about publicity, Latvian rights, etc.? Do you want to want to be talking to film companies? You need a filter. The publishers need the literary agents as a filter as well. They need to know that a submission from Curtis Brown means it's going to be quality, so they had better to respond to it quickly. If you don't go through Curtis Brown, or another good agency, it may end up on their desk for six weeks, eight weeks. Once something is on your desk for six or eight weeks, it's a problem - it's an in tray problem rather than a dynamic submission. Literary agents spend a lot of time sending out the right projects so that the publishers trust us.

Do I need an agent to get a book deal?

Well, 99 percent of all books now are done through literary agents. I would say that you really do need an agent. That obviously makes it tougher for the new writer because they have to go through this filter first, when they may be thinking, 'Why don't I just go to publishers? Why are these people in the middle stopping me from being published?' But, there is a reason why agenting works. It works in New York, it works all over Europe, and it works in England, because publishers trust and need this process. They need literary agents to filter it through.

Can an agent guarantee me a book deal?

Having a literary agent will not guarantee anything. However, if you get the right agent, their hit rate is 60-75% of what they send out sells. I think that's as good as it gets. As an agent, if you don't have many rejections through the year, they're not doing their job properly, because they've got to take risks. We're about finding new voices. Fundamentally, a literary agent has to start from the point of view that they passionately believe in this person's work. It's not throwing things against the wall and seeing what sticks. It's absolutely understanding that this has got to be published. If a publisher rejects you, just think that they're wrong and you're moving on.

Will an agent help me secure a better deal?

Absolutely, categorically, an agent will get you a better deal than being on your own. There's much evidence to prove that this is true. That's not to say that publishers are unscrupulous or will try to con you, and publishers contracts with authors are getting a bit better. However, there is no way that you will understand the complexities of high discount clauses, and what is going on in the marketplace, what is going on in bookshops that dictates publishers values on royalties and on advances. That's why an agent will get you a better contract and will obviously negotiate a higher advance.

Will an agent edit my work?

It was very rare that agents ever edited manuscripts, whereas now it seems to be the norm, and certainly you will find half the job as an agent is getting the manuscript into shape. If any work comes to and it's sixty percent there, the agent has to get it to ninety percent, and the author then has to make the decision of whether trust the agent, or to do that work without any money with that hope of being published.

What is the slush pile?

The slush pile is a not very pleasant way of describing the unsolicited manuscripts that will be received through the reception area at any publishing company. These are the 'Dear Sir/Madams' and the 'Dear Publisher'. The slush pile is made up of the people who are sending in their manuscripts and their proposals hoping that they will be read by someone in the firm. We will receive many of them a month. To be able to judge five or six terrific novels a day is obviously impossible so we have to be highly subjective and very, very decisive. I'm sure we will make wrong decisions sometimes but if the author showed care about knowing what kind of books we want or one of our colleagues wants then it helps them.

LITERARY AGENT

Publishers

At the end of the day, it's impossible for a writer to know what publishers want, which is why the BIG SIX publishers no longer review unsolicited manuscripts, and recommend that serious authors seek the help of agents. Publishers want well-presented manuscripts that are professional in their execution. That means clean white A4 paper, crisp black ink, in a plain font (like Courier) at 12 point. They want double line spacing (or sometimes one-and-a-half), and page numbers at the top right hand side of the header, which contains the book title and your surname for easy identification. They want a manuscript free of typos, spelling and grammatical errors because if you're writing in English it's always exciting to find someone who's got a clue about pesky things like punctuation and clauses. Reading is, after all, an exercise in communication. In short, publishers want to see a manuscript that takes them seriously, (as do agents) (so nothing cute, it reeks of amateur) and shows that you take yourself seriously too – which also means you've done your homework and you're not submitting a paranormal thriller adventure to an editor who handles literary fiction.

Once you've demonstrated that you've mastered the basics, publishers are looking for a story that won't let them stop reading. A page-turner. A story that screams 'buy me or spend the rest of your life regretting it and, quite possibly, unemployed!' One that neatly fits the definition of the kind of story (women's fiction, literary, crime etc) you say yours is. When you're writing genre, in particular, you need to show you understand its rules … especially if you intend to bend or break them. When it comes to the tricky question of working out what a publisher wants. You can't. So you have to please yourself. You have to write the story that gets you all excited about reading, and trust that somewhere out there is an editor (or an agent) who gets excited about the same stories you do. Perseverance is so important in this game. Getting rejected isn't always about the quality of the work. Sometimes it's just a matter of tastes not coinciding. Sometimes an editor loves it but they can't make a good enough case to marketing. Sometimes they've just bought something that's too close to what you've done. Sometimes Saturn is in Pisces and there's a bad moon on the rise.

Self-Publishing

Upon completing your manuscript, it is highly suggested that an editor and a copy-editor be hired to make sure that your book is flowing properly and that the context is grammatically correct. You need to do more than just a spell-check when you have decided to share your works with the world. Self-publishing can be just as rewarding as having one of the Big Six pick your book up, if you are financially ready to take on the task, and you have done your homework.

1. EDITING

An editor will make sure that your work is flowing properly. There are some editors that will do both the editing and copy-editing for one price, but there are just a few of those. In which case, you should prepare to have to pay a copy-editor to do a line by line check of your works for punctuation, grammar and consistency.

Costs:
$45-65/hour based on the experience of the editor
70,000/250 = 280 pages
280 pages /5 pages per hour = 56 hours
Low end is 56 x $45 = $2,520
High end is = $18,200

2. COPY-EDITING

Costs:
2-10 manuscript pages/hour
$25-50/hour based on the experience of the editor
Low end: $840
High end: $7,000 (if it needs a lot of work)

3. COVER DESIGN

The truth is readers do judge a book by its cover. It is important that your cover speak volumes. A standard cover can cost for $50. to $300, depending on the complexity of the cover setup.

If you want to hire someone to make a custom cover design, you can expect to pay anywhere from $150 to $3,500. The higher end is for award-winning designers.

Costs:
Low end: $50
High end: $3,500

4. CONVERSIONS

Print-on-demand conversions for as little as $150 or as much as $2,500 to convert from Word or InDesign. The costs will usually be $200 for a text book that's less than 400 pages. The higher costs are if your original file is in PDF, has a lot of pictures, or is highly illustrated. PDFs are much more complex to convert.

Costs:
Low end: Free
High end: $2,500 or more based on interactivity and pages, according to book design maven Joel Friedlander.

5. GETTING AN ISBN

An ISBN (International Standard Book Number) is recommended if you're doing a print book or want it placed in a library. A lot of third parties sell ISBNs, but if you don't purchase your own ISBN you may not be listed as the publisher of your own work! Not everyone believes you need an ISBN. If you plan on only selling your book in e-book form, then you do have the option of skipping the ISBN and using the default numbering system for Amazon, iBooks or BN.

Costs:
$125 for one ISBN
10 ISBNs for $250
Bowker is the authorized ISBN retailer in the U.S.

6. DISTRIBUTION

You can do this yourself by following the instructions to get your books distributed into the various retailers. However, if you use a third party they do take a percentage of each book sold.
• Amazon distribution instructions
• Barnes and Noble distribution instructions

- Apple iBooks distribution instructions
- Kobo distribution instructions

7. PREPARING YOUR BOOK FOR PRINTING

You no longer have to pay upfront for printing costs because now there are so many print-on-demand options. With print-on-demand services your book only gets printed when someone buys it. It's also not recommended to print books if you don't already have a distribution deal in place. Otherwise, you might end up housing 1,000 books in your garage.

8. GETTING REVIEWS PRE-PUBLICATION

There are many resources for authors to get professional reviews. Sites like Kirkus, Blue Ink, and Publishers Weekly all sell review packages for indie or self-published authors. There's also a great list of bloggers that you can reach out to for reviews for your book.

- Cost of review from Kirkus: $425
- Cost of review from BlueInk Reviews: $396
- Cost of review from Publishers Weekly PW Select: $149

9. MARKETING & PR

This is probably the toughest part after you've written the book. You can pay someone to help you market and set up blog tours for $10 to $40 per hour. For $10 you can get a college student, for $40 to $65 an hour you can get a professional marketer. We recommend you pay someone at least 10 hours to market and on the high end 40 hours. If you have the time, you can do a lot of the marketing yourself. Also, good book publicists can get you radio spots and press pickups for anywhere from $1,000 to $5,000 per month.

Costs:
Low end: $100
High end: $5,000 and up.

The information provided may be somewhat overwhelming.   Review the information, calculate your potential cost, and in some instances it may be more cost effective to research a good and trustworthy self-publishing company that will give you all the services listed above at a better cost.

SELF PUBLISHING

Publicist

A publicist is a person whose job it is to generate and manage publicity for a public figure, especially a celebrity, a business, or for a work such as a book, film or album. Most top-level publicists work in private practice, handling multiple clients.

You may want to use the services of a manager, agent or publicist to help you find work and negotiate pay and work conditions. Some people choose to employ all three types of talent management services, while others use only a manager or only an agent. Each charges a different amount for his services and performs a somewhat different role in your career.

Agent

An agent is responsible for helping you find work and for negotiating the terms of your employment. For example, if you are an actor, your agent keeps his eye out for roles that would be suitable for you and contacts the casting director to arrange auditions. Once a director hires you, your agent will help negotiate your contract and make sure the terms and conditions of your contract are met. You will have a legally binding contract with your agent, allowing him to negotiate on your behalf. Agents are usually paid a percentage of your fees for each job, generally between 10 percent and 15 percent. In California, agent fees are limited to 10 percent of your earnings.

Manager

A manager provides career guidance and advice. Managers may also provide financial and legal advice, if they are qualified to do so. While agents may have hundreds of clients, managers generally have only a few clients but spend more time with each one. A manager's duties are far-ranging and may include advising you on what jobs to take, helping you to market yourself, organizing advertising and publicity, advising on how to develop your talents, making travel arrangements and advising on how to manage your income. Managers generally earn between 15 percent and 20 percent of your total income.

Publicist

A publicist helps you manage your relationship with the media. This may include arranging interviews with journalists; making press announcements on your behalf; organizing your blog, twitter posts or other social media; helping you to gain publicity; arranging for public appearances; and advising on how to avoid unwanted publicity. Publicists often work for large firms and are generally paid a flat fee rather than a percentage of your income. Some publicists work on retainer, whereby the publicist earns a monthly fee for a set amount of work, such as 20 hours a week.

Whom to Hire

Many artists do not feel the need to hire an agent, a manager and a publicist. Some hire all three as well as personal assistants, brand manager, financial manager and lawyer. For example, in 2008, hip hop star 50 Cent earned approximately $150 million and employed a manager, a brand manager, a publicist and an attorney, as well as a vice president and chief operating officer for his record label. For those just starting out, an agent is probably the most important, as it is the agent's job to find you work.

P
U
B
L
I
C
I
S
T

Marketing

The management process through which goods and services move from concept to the customer. It includes the coordination of four elements called the 4Ps of marketing:

1. Identification, selection and development of a product
2. Determination of its price
3. Selection of a distribution channel to reach the customer's place
4. Development and implementation of promotional strategy

For example, new Apple products are developed to include improved applications and systems, are set at different prices depending on how much capability the customer desires, and are sold in places where other Apple products are sold. In order to promote the device, the company featured its debut at tech events and is highly advertised on the web and on television.

Marketing is based on thinking about the business in terms of customer needs and their satisfaction. Marketing differs from selling because (in the words of Harvard Business school's retired professor of marketing Theodore C. Levitt) "Selling concerns itself with the tricks and techniques of getting people to exchange their cash for your product. It is not concerned with the values that the exchange is all about, and it does not, as marketing invariable does, view the entire business process as consisting of a tightly integrated effort to discover, create, arouse and satisfy customer needs." In other words, marketing has less to do with getting customers to pay for your product as it does developing a demand for that product and fulfilling the customer's needs.

Read more:
http://www.businessdictionary.com/definition/marketing.html#ixzz3caxRJwcM

Types of Books

Non-Fiction　　　　*Non-Fiction*　　　　*Fiction*

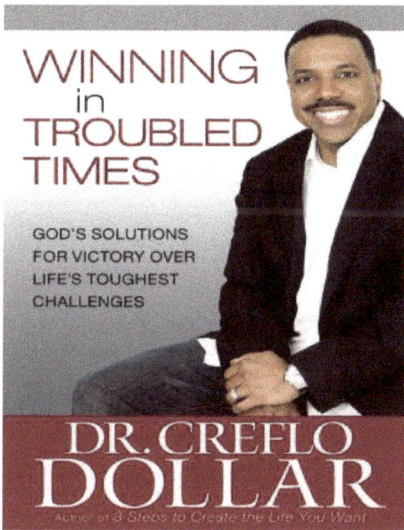  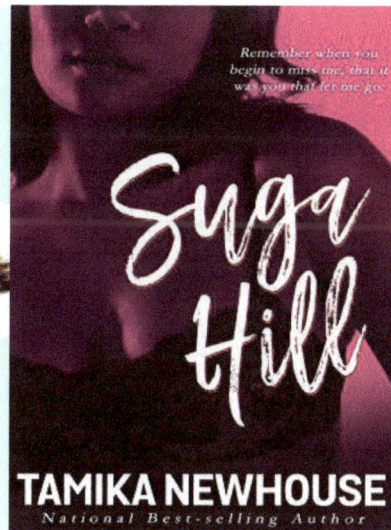

Religion & Spirituality　　*Reference/Self-Help*　　*Romance*

No one chooses the genre of the writer, but only the writer! Writers are not limited to one genre, but they usually stick to the one that mostly peaks their interest, and the interest of their potential audience.

List of Book Genres

Fiction Genre List

Action and Adventure

Chick Literature

Children's

Commercial Fiction

Contemporary

Crime

Erotica

Family Saga

Fantasy

Dark Fantasy

Gay and Lesbian

General Fiction

Graphic Novels

Historical Fiction

Horror

Humor

Literary Fiction

Picture Books

Religious and Inspirational

Romance

Science Fiction

Short Story Collections

Thrillers and Suspense

Western

Women's Fiction

Young Adult

Non-Fiction Genre List

Art & Photography
Biography & Memoirs
Business & Finance
Celebrity & Pop Culture
Music, Film & Entertainment
Cookbooks
Cultural/Social Issues
Current Affairs & Politics
Food & Lifestyle
Gardening
Gay & Lesbian
General Non-Fiction
History & Military
Home Decorating & Design
How To
Humor & Gift Books
Journalism

Juvenile
Medical, Health & Fitness
Multicultural
Narrative
Nature & Ecology
Parenting
Pets
Psychology
Reference
Relationship & Dating
Religion & Spirituality
Science & Technology
Self-Help
Sports
Travel
True Adventure & True Crime
Women's Issues

The Big Six Publishing Companies

HACHETTE BOOK GROUP--the largest publishing company in France, and the second largest publisher in the world.

Hachette Imprints -- has acquired a number of publishing brands aimed at different markets, and these brands themselves contain sub-imprints which are used to publish to an even more targeted audience. Imprints include:

Imprint Name	Market	Notes
Center Street	Traditional values	Main publishing division
FaithWords	Christian Inspirational	Main publishing division
Grand Central Publishing	General market and best-sellers	Formerly Warner Books, has several imprints
5-Spot	Women's fiction	Imprint of Grand Central Publishing
Business Plus	Business publications	Imprint of Grand Central Publishing
Forever	Romance novels	Imprint of Grand Central Publishing
Grand Central Life & Style	Lifestyle & wellness	Imprint of Grand Central Publishing
Twelve	Various	Publishes one book per month that aspires to be high quality; imprint of

Imprint Name	Market	Notes
		Grand Central Publishing
Vision	Various	Mass-market, "blockbuster" products; imprint of Grand Central Publishing
Hachette Digital	Audiobooks & digital books	Publishes Hachette Audio
Little, Brown and Company	American fiction and non-fiction	Focuses on "works of lasting significance"; published Little Women; one of the oldest publishers in the United States
Back Bay Books	Trade paperbacks of fiction and non-fiction including classics and literature	Imprint of Little, Brown and Company
Reagan Arthur Books	Great writing in the service of great stories, http://www.reaganarthurbooks.com	Imprint of Little, Brown and Company
Mulholland Books	Publishes crime novels, thrillers, police procedurals, spy stories, supernatural suspense, http://www.mulhollandbooks.com/	Imprint of Little, Brown and Company
Little, Brown Books for Young Readers	Picture books, hard and softcover fiction and non-fiction for young readers	Has several imprints

H
A
C
H
E
T
T
E

HACHETTE

Imprint Name	Market	Notes
LB Kids	Novelty and brand tie-ins	Imprint of Little, Brown Books for Young Readers
Poppy	Teen Girls	Imprint of Little, Brown Books for Young Readers; publishes the series: Gossip Girl, Poseur, It Girl, The A-List, Secrets of My Hollywood Life, and the Clique.
Orbit Books	Science fiction and fantasy http://www.orbitbooks.net/	
Yen Press	Graphic novels and manga	An imprint of Orbit Books [14]

HARPERCOLLINS is one of the world's largest publishing companies. Headquartered in New York City, the company is a subsidiary of News Corporation.

Imprint Name	Notes
Amistad	Primarily books of African Americans interest, names for the storied ship LaAmistad
Avon	
• Avon Inspire	
• Avon Red	
• Avon Romance	
Balzer+Bray	
Broadside Books	
Caedmon	Audiobooks
• Collins	
Ecco	
• Fourth Estate	Children's literature
• Grafton Books	
• Greenwillow Books	
Harper	
• Harper Audio	
• Harper Business	
• Harper Design	
• Harper Festival	
• Harper Paperbacks	
• Harper Perennial	Originally Perennial Library
• Harper Perennial Modern Classics	
Harper Prism	Science Fiction imprint (merged with Eos)
• HarperCollins Children's Audio	
• HarperCollins Children's Books	
• Harper Collins e-Books	

Imprint Name	Notes
HarperCollins Speakers Bureau	
• HarperLuxe	
• HarperOne	Science fiction imprint (merged with Eos)
• HarperTeen	
• HarperVoyager	
• It Books	
• Mischief	All digital erotica imprint
William Morrow	
• Morrow Cookbooks	
• Katherine Tegen Books	A highly respected series of cookbooks
• Rayo	
Thomas Nelson	Acquired of 2012
• Voyager	
Walden Pond Press	
Zondervan	Acquired evangelical Christian publisher

HARPER COLLINS

MacMILLAN -- is a privately held international publishing company owned by Georg von Holtzbrinck Publishing Group. It has offices in 41 countries worldwide and operates in more than thirty others.

The company is made up of over 50 different divisions operating in five area of publishing:

Education publishing	Including English Language teaching (as Macmillan Education)
Academic publishing	Including reference (as Palgrave Macmillan)
Science, technological and medical publishing	(As Nature Publishing Group), including Nature and other journals
Fiction and non-fiction book publishing	(As Pan Macmillan) under the imprints Pan Books, Picador, Macmillan New Writing, Papermac, Kingfisher, Macmillan Sidgwick & Jackson, Campbell Books, Boxtree, Ltd., and Macmillan Children's Books
MPS Limited	Provides publishing solutions from print and digital publishing solutions, to advert creation, and magazine production, to fulfilment solutions for books and journals.
Publishing Services through MPS Technologies	Offering Content Delivery, Web analytics, and Technology related services, as well as distribution and production.

M
A
C
M
I
L
L
A
N

PENGUIN -- Penguin Books is now the flagship imprint of the worldwide Penguin Group and is owned by Pearson PLC, the global media company who also own the Financial Times, the business information group and Pearson, the world's largest education publishing and technology company.

Alien Lane	In 1967 Penguin's founder started an eponymous hardback imprint under the name of Allen Lane. This now has a dynamic, growing list and publishes accessible and quality non-fiction books of lasting value.
Penguin Classics	In January 1946, the Penguin Classics list was launched with E. V. Rieu's translation of The Odyssey. The series now consists of over 800 titles including the best in English, American, European, classical and non-western literature and an extensive range of philosophy, religion, art, history and politics titles.
Particular Books	The Particular Books imprint was launched in 2009. This list is characterized by the particular, all-consuming passions of its unique authors for a whole range of subjects that fascinate many of us, such as music, numbers, French cooking, gardening, cycling, survival tactics, books, clothes and maps of remote islands.
Reference	Penguin is one of the best-known names in reference publishing with an astonishingly rich list that extends from Roget's Thesaurus and Pears Cyclopaedia to dictionaries on subjects as diverse as psychology, science, symbols and saints.
Michael Joseph	An imprint of Penguin, publishes highly commercial, popular fiction and non-fiction, principally interested in publishing Top Ten Bestsellers. Michael Joseph is at the cutting edge of the commercial book world, publishing engaging fiction and fast and reactive non-fiction, giving our readers what they really want.
Fiction	Our fiction publishing includes: crime and thrillers, contemporary women's fiction, romance and humor; alongside boys' adventure, fantasy and historical novels. Amongst our bestselling fiction authors are: Marian Keyes, Jane Green, Catherine Alliott, Clive Cussler, Sue Townsend Dick Francis, Nicci French, Eliza-

Ibeth Noble, Lesley Pearse, Jane Fallon.

Non-Fiction	The non fiction list embraces celebrity autobiography and show-biz, including memoirs by Stephen Fry, Michael McIntyre and Ant and Dec. We also publish into sport, popular history, health and current affairs, with bestseller upon bestseller by Jeremy Clarkson.

Our cookery list boasts regular bestsellers from Jamie Oliver and we are proud to celebrate the successes of our other cookery authors too, including Elizabeth David the popular River Café series, headed by chefs Rose Gray and Ruth Rogers and cookbook Economy Gastronomy, by chefs Allegra McEvedy and Paul Merrett.

Penguin General

Penguin Paperbacks

The first ten paperback Penguin books appeared in 1935 costing 6d each (the price of a packet of cigarettes). Since then the Penguin list has developed enormously, but still aims to bring the best writing to the widest possible audience. Penguin Paperbacks now range from Booker Prize-winning contemporary authors, to mass market bestsellers, with successful history, biography and general non-fiction as well.

Hamish Hamilton

Founded in 1931, Hamish Hamilton is one of Britain's most distinguished literary lists. Now an integral part of Penguin, it provides a home for an exciting and eclectic group of authors, united by the distinctiveness and excellence of their writing. Publishing no more than twenty new titles a year, both fiction and non-fiction, and all points in between, Hamish Hamilton's authors include Ali Smith, Mohsin Hamid, Arundhati Roy, Noam Chomsky, Jonathan Safran Foer, Kiran Desai, Dave Eggers, W.G. Sebald, Iain Sinclair, Roger Deakin, Zadie Smith, Alain de Botton, James Kelman, Hari Kunzru, David Foster Wallace, Susan Sontag and John Updike.

Hamish Hamilton also publishes the (almost) monthly literary magazine Five Dials, edited by Craig Taylor and launched in

2008. Back issues are archived and downloadable/printable for free at www.fivedials.com.

Its staff are: Simon Prosser, Juliette Mitchell, Anna Kelly, and Craig Taylor.

Viking

Viking publishes the widest possible range of literary fiction and non-fiction. Our fiction list includes John le Carré, Nick Hornby, Will Self, Colm Tóibín, Nicole Krauss, William Trevor, Catherine O' Flynn, Jonathan Coe, and Joshua Ferris. In non-fiction, the range covers current affairs, history, biography, memoir, narrative non-fiction, music and sport. Our authors include Antony Beevor, Andrew Rawnsley, Mark Bostridge, Sarah Bradford, Saul David, Catherine Bailey, Lynn Barber, Claire Tomalin and John Stubbs.

Fig Tree

Fig Tree was set up in 2005 and its aim is to publish a list of well written, entertaining, and distinct books. The list is mostly fiction but also publishes history, biography, memoir, and tongue in cheek or off kilter how-to. Bestselling and award winning authors include: Marina Lewycka, Zoe Heller, India Knight, Anita Brookner, Patrick Neate, Martin Gayford, Alex Kapranos, Miranda Carter, Penelope Lively, Rachel Johnson, Kathryn Stockett and Julie Kavanagh.

Penguin Audiobooks

Penguin Audiobooks was launched in 1993, and over 300 titles are now available. Our list reflects the publishing diversity of the Penguin book range and includes contemporary and classic fiction, autobiography, crime, history, and non-fiction from authors such as Marian Keyes, Ian Fleming, Niall Ferguson, Antony Beevor, Marina Lewycka, Nick Hornby and Zadie Smith.

Penguin Audiobooks are available on CD and also as downloadable eAudiobooks.

| Puffin | In Puffin n Audiobooks we publish the best in contemporary and classic literature for younger listeners. Our authors include Roald Dahl, Eoin Colfer, Charlie Higson, Rick Riordan, Lynley Dodd and Lauren Child. Our narrators include Simon Callow, Martin Jarvis, Stephen Fry, Adrian Dunbar, Timothy West, Juliet Stevenson, Richard E Grant, Nicholas Hoult, Paul Whitehouse, and Will Young. |

| ePenguin | September 2001 saw the launch of ePenguin, a range of ebooks that reflects the breadth and integrity of the Penguin catalogue. Packed with the best in fiction, science writing, business titles, reference books and a full selection of Penguin Classics and Rough Guides, ePenguin extends the Penguin tradition of innovative, quality publishing into the digital age. |

Children's Division

| Puffin | Puffin is the UK's leading publisher of children's books and one of its best-loved brands. The publishing program spans novelty books for the very young and picture books through to teenage fiction, and poetry and non-fiction through to film and TV tie-ins. Puffin publishes an award-winning range of bestselling authors including Janet & Allan Ahlberg, Eric Carle, Eoin Colfer, Roald Dahl, Anne Fine, Dick King-Smith and Melvin Burgess. |

| Warne | Frederick Warne was founded in 1865 by a bookseller turned publisher who gave his own name to the firm and is the home of our classic brands. Warne's best-known author was Beatrix Potter, creator of the world-famous Peter Rabbit Books. Since its acquisition by Penguin in 1983, Warne has focused on the development of Beatrix Potter and the acquisition of other book-based children's character properties; including Cicely Mary Barker's Flower Fairies,in 1989 and Eric Hill's Spot in 1993. The hallmarks of the publishing program are beautifully produced editions of the original works, plus lively spin-off books ranging from baby record books and treasuries to board books and novelty titles. Today Warne manages an international program of publishing, licensing and entertainment. |

PENGUIN

PENGUIN

Ladybird

During the First World War, Wills and Hepworth a small commercial printer in Loughborough, Leicestershire, began to produce children's books under the imprint Ladybird. In 1940 the now-familiar 'pocket-sized' Ladybird book or mini-hardback was first produced for a series of animal stories. Nearly seventy years later, the original principles of Ladybird remains, to provide children with entertaining, engaging and educational books, whilst offering great value for money and the very best in innovative formats. The list today includes first books for babies, novelty books, sound books and the latest in exciting new film and television licenses. Our aim is to always put the child at the centre of everything we do, whatever their interest and stage of development using the latest develops and findings in educational research to influence our publishing.

BBC Children's Books

Penguin formed a joint venture with BBC Worldwide in 2004 and since then BBC Children's Books has gone on to publish some of the most well known, contemporary children's brands. Supporting the most popular and best-performing BBC programs, these include number 1 preschool children's property In the Night Garden, popular family show Top Gear and the huge cult hit Doctor Who. By publishing a range of innovative formats at unbeatable price points, BBC Children's Books have consistently remained at the top of the children's book charts.

Dorling Kindersley

Is an international publishing company specializing in the creation of high quality, illustrated information books, interactive software, TV programs and online resources for children and adults.

RANDOM HOUSE ("RH") -- is the largest general-interest trade book publisher in the world. It has been owned since 1998 by the German private media corporation Bertelsmann and has become the umbrella brand for Bertelsmann book publishing.

Random House, U.S.A. Imprints

Crown Publishing Group
- Amphoto Books
- Back Stage Books
- Billboard Books
- Broadway
- Broadway Business
- Clarkson Potter
- Crown
- Crown Business
- Crown Forum
- Doubleday Religion
- Harmony Books
- Hogarth Press
- Potter Craft
- Potter Style
- Ten Speed Press
- Three Rivers Press
- Tricycle Press
- Shaye Areheart Books
- WaterBrook Multnomah
- Watson-Guptill

Knopf Doubleday Publishing Group
- Alfred A. Knopf
- Anchor Books
- Doubleday
- Everyman's Library
- Nan A. Talese
- Pantheon Books
- Schocken Books
- Vintage

RH Publishing Group
- Ballantine Books
- Bantam
- Delacorte
- Del Rey
- Del Rey / Lucas

Books
- Dell
- The Dial Press
- Kodansha Comics

USA
- The Modern Library
- One World
- Presido Press
- RH Trade Group
- RH Trade Paperbacks
- Spectra
- Spiegel & Grau
- Villard Books

RH Value Publishing
- Children's Classics
- Crescent Books
- Derrydale
- Gramercy Books
- Testament Books
- Wings Books

RH Children's Books
- RH Children's Books (Kids@Random)
- Beginner Books
- David Fickling Books
- Nickelodeon Books (2012-)
- Delacorte Press
- Golden Books
- Prima Games
- Step Into Reading
- Schwartz & Wade
- Stepping Stone Books
- Sylvan Learning
- Wendy Lamb Books

Digital Publishing Group
- Fodor's Travel
- Listening Library
- Living Language
- Princeton Review
- RH Audio
- RH Large Print

Random House International Imprints

The RH Group
Cornerstone Publishing
- Arrow
- Century
- William Heinemann
- Hutchinson
- Preface
- RH Books
- RH

Business Books
- RH Audio
- Tanoshimi Manga
- Windmill

Vintage Publishing
- Chatto & Windus
- Harvill Secker
- Jonathan Cape
- Pimlico
- Square Peg
- The Bodley Head
- Vintage Classics
- Yellow Jersey

Ebury Publishing
- BBC Books
- Ebury Press
- Vermilion
- Rider
- Time Out Books
- Virgin Books

Transworld Publishers
- Corgi
- Bantam
- Black Swan
- Channel 4
- Doubleday
- Eden Project
- Expert
- Transworld Ireland
- Transworld Sport

RH Children's Publishers
UK
- Bantam
- Jonathan Cape
- Corgi
- David Fickling Books
- Doubleday
- Eden Project
- Red Fox
- Hutchinson
- Tamarind
- The Bodley Head

Mainstream Publishing

RH Australia

Rand RH India

Rand RH New Zealand

RH Struik

Verlagsgruppe RH
- Adeo
- Ansata
- Jugendbücher
- cbt Jugendbücher
- Der Hörverlag
- Diana
- Diederichs
- DVA
- Edition Elke Heidenreich
- Gerth Medien
- Goldmann
- Gütersloher Verlagshaus
- Heyne
- Integral
- Irisiana
- Kailash
- Knaus
- Kösel
- Limes
- Lotos
- Luchterhand Literaturverlag
- Ludwig
- Manesse
- Manhattan
- Mosaik bei Goldmann
- Paige & Turner
- Pantheon
- Penhaligon
- Prestel
- RH Audio
- RH

Random House International Imprints (Cont'd)

Entertainment
- Riemann
- Siedler
- Sphinx
- Südwest
- Tag & Nacht

Ariston
- Arkana
- Bassermann
- Blanvalet
- Blessing
- btb
- carl's books
- C. Bertelsmann
- cbj audio
- cbj avanti
- cbj Kinder- und Jugendbücher
- cbt Jugendbücher
- Der Hörverlag
- Diana
- Diederichs
- DVA
- Edition Elke Heidenreich
- Gerth Medien
- Goldmann
- Gütersloher Verlagshaus
- Heyne
- Integral
- Irisiana
- Kailash
- Knaus

- Kösel
- Limes
- Lotos
- Luchterhand Literaturverlag
- Ludwig
- Manesse
- Manhattan
- Mosaik bei Goldmann
- Paige & Turner
- Pantheon
- Penhaligon
- Prestel
- RH Audio
- RH

Entertainment
- Riemann
- Siedler
- Sphinx
- Südwest
- Tag & Nacht

RH Mondadori
- Areté
- Caballo de Troya
- Collins
- Debate
- DeBolsillo
- Electa
- Grijalbo
- Grijalbo Ilustrados
- Lumen
- Lumen Infantil
- Mondadori
- Montena

- Plaza & Janés
- Rosa dels Vents
- Sudamericana

RH of Canada
The Knopf Random Canada Publishing Group
- Knopf Canada
- RH Canada
- Seal Books
- Vintage Canada

The McClelland & Stewart Doubleday Canada Publishing Group
- Anchor Canada
- Appetite by RH
- Bond Street
- Doubleday Canada
- Douglas Gibson

Books
- Emblem
- Tundra Books
- Journey Prize Stories
- New Canadian Library

SIMON & SCHUSTER – division of CBS Corporation, is a publisher founded in New York City in 1924 by Richard L. Simon and M. Lincoln ("Max") Schuster. It is one of the four largest English-language publishers and publishing houses.

Imprint	Notes
Adults:	
Atria	
Atria Espanol	
Beyond Words Publishing	Specializes in publishing new age, self help, and inspiration stories with a spiritual focus.
Emily Bestler Books	
Fireside Books	
Free Press	
Gallery Books	
Howard Books	
Pocket Books	
Scribner	
Strebor	
Touchstone	
Threshold Editions	Specializes in publishing politically right-of-center books, including Jerome R. Corsi's controversial The Obama Nation.
Washington Square Press	
Cash Money Content	
Mercury Ink	
Young Adults and Children:	
Aladdin	
Atheneum	Initially (1959) a publishing house and adult imprint it now publishes children's titles formerly just part of its output.
Beach Lane Books	
Little Simon	
Margaret K. McElderry Books[8]	
Paula Wiseman	
Simon & Schuster Books for Young Readers	
Simon Pulse, Simon Spotlight	

1. WWW.BUSINESSDICTIONARY.COM

2. WORLDWIDE INTERNET

3. SEVERAL BLOG SITES FOR AUTHORS, SUCH AS:

    a. The Future of Ink
    b. Books and Such
    c. Jeff Goins
    d. Write to Done
    e. The Book Designer
    f. Jody Hedlund
    g. Jane Friedman

Though every effort has been made to ensure the information in this publication is reliable, 3G Publishing, Inc. does not guarantee the accuracy of the data contained herein. All information should be verified to make sure that it is consistent with and applicable to your publishing needs.

Note: Big six companies listed with their imprints may have increased imprints or may have removed some that are currently in this guide, due to the changes that occur on a daily basis in the publishing industry.

www.ingramcontent.com/pod-product-compliance
Lightning Source LLC
Chambersburg PA
CBHW041426270326
41931CB00023B/3497